Morning and Evening Prayer
on Sunday

Church House Publishing

Published by	Church House Publishing
	Church House
	Great Smith Street
	London SW1P 3NZ

Printed and bound by ArklePrint Ltd, Northampton on 80 gsm Dutchman Ivory

Typeset in Gill Sans by John Morgan and Shirley Thompson/Omnific Designed by Derek Birdsall RDI

The material in this booklet is extracted from *Common Worship: Services and Prayers for the Church of England*. It comprises:

¶   Morning and Evening Prayer on Sunday;
¶   extracts from Prayers for Various Occasions;
¶   The Litany;
¶   extracts from Canticles;
¶   extracts from A Service of the Word;
¶   General Rules.

For other material, page references to *Common Worship: Services and Prayers for the Church of England* are supplied.

Pagination   This booklet has two sets of page numbers. The outer numbers are the booklet's own page numbers, while the inner numbers near the centre of most pages refer to the equivalent pages in *Common Worship: Services and Prayers for the Church of England*.

Contents

Authorization

¶   The following services comply with the provisions of A Service of the Word (pages 61–66):

   ¶   An Order for Morning Prayer on Sunday

   ¶   An Order for Evening Prayer on Sunday

¶   A Service of the Word and the following material are authorized pursuant to Canon B 2 of the Canons of the Church of England for use until further resolution of the General Synod: Prayers for Various Occasions (except the General Thanksgiving); the Litany; Authorized Forms of Confession and Absolution; the Apostles' Creed; the Lord's Prayer; Opening Canticles at Morning Prayer; Gospel Canticles; Other Canticles; A Song of Praise (Epiphany); Te Deum Laudamus; General Rules.

¶   The General Thanksgiving is taken from *The Book of Common Praye*

¶   The following material has been commended by the House of Bish of the General Synod pursuant to Canon B 2 of the Canons of the Church of England and is published with the agreement of the Hou Phos hilaron – a Song of the Light; Old and New Testament Cantic at Morning and Evening Prayer; Introduction to Morning and Eveni Prayer on Sunday.

   Under Canon B 4 it is open to each bishop to authorize, if he sees fit, the form of service to be used within his diocese. He may speci that the services shall be those commended by the House, or that diocesan form of them shall be used. If the bishop gives no directic in this matter the priest remains free, subject to the terms of Can B 5, to make use of the material as commended by the House.

Morning and Evening Prayer on Sunday

¶ *Introduction*

From earliest times, Christians gathered at regular hours during each day and night to respond to God's word with praise on behalf of all creation and with intercession for the salvation of the world. By the fourth century, if not earlier, morning and evening had emerged as the pre-eminent hours for the offering of this sacrifice of praise. They have remained so ever since, especially on Sundays when the Church commemorates both the first day of creation and the day of Christ's resurrection. These orders of service are examples of forms which comply with the provisions of A Service of the Word and are intended to help Christians of our own day take their part in this privilege and duty which belongs to all God's priestly people. They may be celebrated in a variety of different ways, for example, as:

¶ a simple form of prayer at the very beginning or end of the day;

¶ the Gathering and Liturgy of the Word for another service which is to follow immediately;

¶ the principal service of the day.

To meet diverse needs such as these, they are very flexible in arrangement. The central core, however, consists of the Liturgy of the Word interwoven with canticles to supply the response of praise, followed by intercessory prayer in one form or another. A variety of alternative endings is provided in the form of thanksgivings for different aspects of the Church's life. Whenever possible, the services should include some singing, especially of the Gospel canticle, which is the climax of the morning or evening praise for the work of God in Christ. If desired, metrical paraphrases may be substituted for any of the biblical canticles, and other hymns and songs may be added at appropriate points.

Provision for weekdays is published separately.

For Notes, see pages 28–30.

An Order for Morning Prayer on Sunday

Preparation

Grace, mercy and peace
from God our Father
and the Lord Jesus Christ
be with you

All   **and also with you.**

This is the day that the Lord has made.

All   **Let us rejoice and be glad in it.**

(or)

O Lord, open our lips

All   **and our mouth shall proclaim your praise.**

Give us the joy of your saving help

All   **and sustain us with your life-giving Spirit.**

The minister may say

We have come together in the name of Christ
to offer our praise and thanksgiving,
to hear and receive God's holy word,
to pray for the needs of the world,
and to seek the forgiveness of our sins,
that by the power of the Holy Spirit
we may give ourselves to the service of God.

Prayers of Penitence are used when Morning Prayer is the principal
service and may be used on other occasions (see Note 3).

The following or another authorized confession and absolution is used

Jesus says, 'Repent, for the kingdom of heaven is close at hand.'
So let us turn away from our sin and turn to Christ,
confessing our sins in penitence and faith.

All **Lord God,**
we have sinned against you;
we have done evil in your sight.
We are sorry and repent.
Have mercy on us according to your love.
Wash away our wrongdoing and cleanse us from our sin.
Renew a right spirit within us
and restore us to the joy of your salvation;
through Jesus Christ our Lord. Amen.

May the Father of all mercies
cleanse *you* from *your* sins,
and restore *you* in his image
to the praise and glory of his name,
through Jesus Christ our Lord.

All **Amen.**

Blessed is the Lord,
All **for he has heard the voice of our prayer;**

therefore shall our hearts dance for joy
All **and in our song will we praise our God.**

One or more of the following may conclude the Preparation or they may be omitted.

This prayer of thanksgiving may be said

Blessed are you, Lord our God,
creator and redeemer of all;
to you be glory and praise for ever.
From the waters of chaos you drew forth the world
and in your great love fashioned us in your image.
Now, through the deep waters of death,
you have brought your people to new birth
by raising your Son to life in triumph.
May Christ your light ever dawn in our hearts
as we offer you our sacrifice of thanks and praise.
Blessed be God, Father, Son and Holy Spirit:

All **Blessed be God for ever.**

An opening canticle or a hymn may be said or sung.

This opening prayer may be said

The night has passed, and the day lies open before us;
let us pray with one heart and mind.

Silence is kept.

As we rejoice in the gift of this new day,
so may the light of your presence, O God,
set our hearts on fire with love for you;
now and for ever.

All **Amen.**

The Word of God

Psalmody

The appointed psalmody is said or sung.

Each psalm or group of psalms may end with

Glory to the Father and to the Son
and to the Holy Spirit;
as it was in the beginning is now
and shall be for ever. Amen.

Old Testament Canticle

*If there are two Scripture readings, the first may be read here,
or both may be read after the Old Testament canticle.*

A suitable canticle is said or sung (see Note 5 on page 29).

Scripture Reading

*One or more readings appointed for the day are read.
The reading(s) may be followed by a time of silence.*

The reader may say

This is the word of the Lord.
All **Thanks be to God.**

*A suitable song or chant, or a responsory in this or another form,
may follow*

Awake, O sleeper, and arise from the dead.
All **And Christ shall give you light.**
You have died and your life is hid with Christ in God.
All **Awake, O sleeper, and arise from the dead.**
Set your minds on things that are above,
    not on things that are on the earth.
All **And Christ shall give you light.**
When Christ our life appears you will appear with him in glory.
All **Awake, O sleeper, and arise from the dead,
    and Christ shall give you light.**

Gospel Canticle

The Benedictus (The Song of Zechariah) is said or sung

1 Blessed be the Lord the God of Israel, ♦
  who has come to his people and set them free.

2 He has raised up for us a mighty Saviour, ♦
  born of the house of his servant David.

3 Through his holy prophets God promised of old ♦
  to save us from our enemies,
      from the hands of all that hate us,

4 To show mercy to our ancestors, ♦
  and to remember his holy covenant.

5 This was the oath God swore to our father Abraham: ♦
  to set us free from the hands of our enemies,

6 Free to worship him without fear, ♦
  holy and righteous in his sight
      all the days of our life.

7 And you, child, shall be called the prophet of the Most High, ♦
  for you will go before the Lord to prepare his way,

8 To give his people knowledge of salvation ♦
  by the forgiveness of all their sins.

9 In the tender compassion of our God ♦
  the dawn from on high shall break upon us,

10 To shine on those who dwell in darkness and the shadow of death,
  and to guide our feet into the way of peace.   *Luke 1.68-*

  Glory to the Father and to the Son
  and to the Holy Spirit;
  as it was in the beginning is now
  and shall be for ever. Amen.

*A sermon is preached when Morning Prayer is the principal service
(see Note 3).*

*Morning Prayer may conclude with one of the Thanksgivings
(pages 18–28).*

The Creed

*When Morning Prayer is the principal service, the Apostles' Creed
or an authorized Affirmation of Faith is said. It may be omitted on other
occasions (see Note 3).*

All **I believe in God, the Father almighty,
creator of heaven and earth.**

**I believe in Jesus Christ, his only Son, our Lord,
who was conceived by the Holy Spirit,
born of the Virgin Mary,
suffered under Pontius Pilate,
was crucified, died, and was buried;
he descended to the dead.
On the third day he rose again;
he ascended into heaven,
he is seated at the right hand of the Father,
and he will come to judge the living and the dead.**

**I believe in the Holy Spirit,
the holy catholic Church,
the communion of saints,
the forgiveness of sins,
the resurrection of the body,
and the life everlasting.
Amen.**

Prayers

Intercessions are offered.

The Collect is said.

The Lord's Prayer is said

Gathering our prayers and praises into one,
as our Saviour has taught us, so we pray

All   **Our Father in heaven,
hallowed be your name,
your kingdom come,
your will be done,
on earth as in heaven.
Give us today our daily bread.
Forgive us our sins
as we forgive those who sin against us.
Lead us not into temptation
but deliver us from evil.
For the kingdom, the power,
and the glory are yours
now and for ever.
Amen.**

(or)

Gathering our prayers and praises into one,
let us pray with confidence as our Saviour has taught us

All   **Our Father, who art in heaven,
hallowed be thy name;
thy kingdom come;
thy will be done;
on earth as it is in heaven.
Give us this day our daily bread.
And forgive us our trespasses,
as we forgive those who trespass against us.
And lead us not into temptation;
but deliver us from evil.
For thine is the kingdom,
the power, and the glory
for ever and ever.
Amen.**

The Conclusion

The service ends with one of the following, or another blessing or ending.

The Blessing

The Lord bless us, and preserve us from all evil,
and keep us in eternal life.

All　**Amen.**

[Let us bless the Lord.

All　**Thanks be to God.**]

(or)

The Grace

All　**The grace of our Lord Jesus Christ,
and the love of God,
and the fellowship of the Holy Spirit,
be with us all evermore.
Amen.**

(or)

The Peace

May the peace of God, which passes all understanding,
keep our hearts and minds in Christ Jesus.

All　**Amen.**

The peace of the Lord be always with you

All　**and also with you.**

These words may be added

Let us offer one another a sign of peace, God's seal on our prayers.

An Order for Evening Prayer on Sunday

The light and peace of Jesus Christ be with you
All **and also with you.**

The glory of the Lord has risen upon us.
All **Let us rejoice and sing God's praise for ever.**

(or)

O God, make speed to save us.
All **O Lord, make haste to help us.**

Lead your people to freedom, O God.
All **And banish all darkness from our hearts and minds.**

The minister may say

We have come together in the name of Christ
to offer our praise and thanksgiving,
to hear and receive God's holy word,
to pray for the needs of the world,
and to seek the forgiveness of our sins,
that by the power of the Holy Spirit
we may give ourselves to the service of God.

*Prayers of Penitence are used when Evening Prayer is the principal
service and may be used on other occasions (see Note 3).*

The following or another authorized confession and absolution is used

Jesus says, 'Repent, for the kingdom of heaven is close at hand.'
So let us turn away from our sin and turn to Christ,
confessing our sins in penitence and faith.

All **Most merciful God,
Father of our Lord Jesus Christ,
we confess that we have sinned
in thought, word and deed.
We have not loved you with our whole heart.
We have not loved our neighbours as ourselves.
In your mercy
forgive what we have been,
help us to amend what we are,
and direct what we shall be;
that we may do justly,
love mercy,
and walk humbly with you, our God.
Amen.**

May the God of love and power
forgive *you* and free *you* from *your* sins,
heal and strengthen *you* by his Spirit,
and raise *you* to new life in Christ our Lord.

All **Amen.**

One or more of the following may conclude the Preparation or they may be omitted.

This prayer of thanksgiving may be said

Blessed are you, sovereign God,
our light and our salvation;
to you be glory and praise for ever.
You led your people to freedom
by a pillar of cloud by day and a pillar of fire by night.
May we who walk in the light of your presence
acclaim your Christ, rising victorious,
as he banishes all darkness from our hearts and minds.
Blessed be God, Father, Son and Holy Spirit:

All **Blessed be God for ever.**

An opening hymn may be sung.

Verses from Psalm 141 or from Psalm 104 may be said (see pages 44–45).

This opening prayer may be said

The day is almost over, and the evening has come;
let us pray with one heart and mind.

Silence is kept.

As our evening prayer rises before you, O God,
so may your Spirit come down upon us
to set us free to sing your praise
for ever and ever.

All **Amen.**

The Word of God

Psalmody

The appointed psalmody is said or sung.

Each psalm or group of psalms may end with

Glory to the Father and to the Son
and to the Holy Spirit;
as it was in the beginning is now
and shall be for ever. Amen.

New Testament Canticle

*If there are two Scripture readings, the first may be read here, or both
may be read after the New Testament canticle.*

A suitable canticle is said or sung (see Note 5 on page 29).

Scripture Reading

*One or more readings appointed for the day are read.
The reading(s) may be followed by a time of silence.*

The reader may say

This is the word of the Lord.

All **Thanks be to God.**

*A suitable song or chant, or a responsory in this or another form,
may follow*

The Lord is my light and my salvation;
    the Lord is the strength of my life.

All **The Lord is my light and my salvation;**
    the Lord is the strength of my life.

The light shines in the darkness
    and the darkness has not overcome it.

All **The Lord is the strength of my life.**

Glory to the Father, and to the Son
    and to the Holy Spirit.

All **The Lord is my light and my salvation;**
    the Lord is the strength of my life.

The Magnificat (The Song of Mary) is said or sung

1   My soul proclaims the greatness of the Lord,
        my spirit rejoices in God my Saviour; ♦
    he has looked with favour on his lowly servant.

2   From this day all generations will call me blessed; ♦
    the Almighty has done great things for me
        and holy is his name.

3   He has mercy on those who fear him, ♦
    from generation to generation.

4   He has shown strength with his arm ♦
    and has scattered the proud in their conceit,

5   Casting down the mighty from their thrones ♦
    and lifting up the lowly.

6   He has filled the hungry with good things ♦
    and sent the rich away empty.

7   He has come to the aid of his servant Israel, ♦
    to remember his promise of mercy,

8   The promise made to our ancestors, ♦
    to Abraham and his children for ever.   *Luke 1.46-*

    Glory to the Father and to the Son
    and to the Holy Spirit;
    as it was in the beginning is now
    and shall be for ever. Amen.

*A sermon is preached when Evening Prayer is the principal service
(see Note 3).*

*Evening Prayer may conclude with one of the Thanksgivings
(pages 18–28).*

The Creed

When Evening Prayer is the principal service, the Apostles' Creed or an authorized Affirmation of Faith is said. It may be omitted on other occasions (see Note 3).

All   **I believe in God, the Father almighty,**
creator of heaven and earth.

I believe in Jesus Christ, his only Son, our Lord,
who was conceived by the Holy Spirit,
born of the Virgin Mary,
suffered under Pontius Pilate,
was crucified, died, and was buried;
he descended to the dead.
On the third day he rose again;
he ascended into heaven,
he is seated at the right hand of the Father,
and he will come to judge the living and the dead.

I believe in the Holy Spirit,
the holy catholic Church,
the communion of saints,
the forgiveness of sins,
the resurrection of the body,
and the life everlasting.
Amen.

Prayers

Intercessions are offered.

The Collect is said.

The Lord's Prayer is said

Gathering our prayers and praises into one,
as our Saviour has taught us, so we pray

All **Our Father in heaven,
hallowed be your name,
your kingdom come,
your will be done,
on earth as in heaven.
Give us today our daily bread.
Forgive us our sins
as we forgive those who sin against us.
Lead us not into temptation
but deliver us from evil.
For the kingdom, the power,
and the glory are yours
now and for ever.
Amen.**

(or)

Gathering our prayers and praises into one,
let us pray with confidence as our Saviour has taught us

All **Our Father, who art in heaven,
hallowed be thy name;
thy kingdom come;
thy will be done;
on earth as it is in heaven.
Give us this day our daily bread.
And forgive us our trespasses,
as we forgive those who trespass against us.
And lead us not into temptation;
but deliver us from evil.
For thine is the kingdom,
the power, and the glory
for ever and ever.
Amen.**

The Conclusion

The service ends with one of the following, or another blessing or ending.

The Blessing

The Lord bless us, and preserve us from all evil,
and keep us in eternal life.

All **Amen.**

[Let us bless the Lord.

All **Thanks be to God.**]

(or)

The Grace

All **The grace of our Lord Jesus Christ,
and the love of God,
and the fellowship of the Holy Spirit,
be with us all evermore.
Amen.**

(or)

The Peace

May the peace of God, which passes all understanding,
keep our hearts and minds in Christ Jesus.

All **Amen.**

The peace of the Lord be always with you

All **and also with you.**

These words may be added

Let us offer one another a sign of peace, God's seal on our prayers.

Thanksgivings for Use at Morning and Evening Prayer on Sunday

¶ *Thanksgiving for the Word*

Your word is a lantern to our feet
All **and a light upon our path.**

This prayer of thanksgiving may be said

Blessed are you, Lord our God.
How sweet are your words to the taste,
sweeter than honey to the mouth.
How precious are your commands for our life,
more than the finest gold in our hands.
How marvellous is your will for the world,
unending is your love for the nations.
Our voices shall sing of your promises
and our lips declare your praise
for ever and ever.
All **Amen.**

After a suitable introduction, this or another authorized confession and
absolution may be used (see Note 3)

All **O King enthroned on high,**
filling the earth with your glory:
holy is your name,
Lord God almighty.
In our sinfulness we cry to you
to take our guilt away,
and to cleanse our lips to speak your word,
through Jesus Christ our Lord.
Amen.

May the God of all healing and forgiveness
draw *us* to himself,
and cleanse *us* from all *our* sins
that *we* may behold the glory of his Son,
the Word made flesh,
Jesus Christ our Lord.
All **Amen.**

Testimonies may be shared. The Apostles' Creed or an authorized Affirmation of Faith is said at a principal service and may be said on other occasions (see Note 3).

Intercessions are offered.

This or another Collect is said

Almighty God,
we thank you for the gift of your holy word.
May it be a lantern to our feet,
a light upon our paths,
and a strength to our lives.
Take us and use us
to love and serve all people
in the power of the Holy Spirit
and in the name of your Son,
Jesus Christ our Lord.

All **Amen.**

The Lord's Prayer is said.

The service ends either with the Peace or with the following proclamation to the world

The Word of life which was from the beginning
All **we proclaim to you.**
The darkness is passing away
and the true light is already shining;
All **the Word of life which was from the beginning.**
That which we heard, which we saw with our eyes,
and touched with our hands,
All **we proclaim to you.**
For our fellowship is with the Father,
and with his Son, Jesus Christ our Lord.
All **The Word of life, which was from the beginning,
we proclaim to you.**

Let us bless the Lord.
All **Thanks be to God.**

¶ *Thanksgiving for Holy Baptism*

If possible, this Thanksgiving should be celebrated at the font.

I saw water flowing from the threshold of the temple.

All **Wherever the river flows**
everything will spring to life. Alleluia.

On the banks of the river grow trees bearing every kind of fruit.

All **Their leaves will not wither nor their fruit fail.**

Their fruit will serve for food,
their leaves for the healing of the nations.

All **For the river of the water of life**
flows from the throne of God and of the Lamb.

This prayer of thanksgiving is said and water may be poured into the font.

God in Christ gives us water welling up for eternal life.
With joy you will draw water from the wells of salvation.

All **Lord, give us this water and we shall thirst no more.**

Let us give thanks to the Lord our God.

All **It is right to give thanks and praise.**

Blessed are you, sovereign God of all,
to you be glory and praise for ever.
You are our light and our salvation.
From the deep waters of death
you have raised your Son to life in triumph.
Grant that all who have been born anew by water and the Spirit,
may daily be renewed in your image,
walk by the light of faith,
and serve you in newness of life;
through your anointed Son, Jesus Christ,
to whom with you and the Holy Spirit
we lift our voices of praise.
Blessed be God, Father, Son and Holy Spirit:

All **Blessed be God for ever.**

The Apostles' Creed or an authorized Affirmation of Faith is said (see Note 3).

Intercessions are offered. These should include prayer for those who are preparing for baptism and for those recently baptized.

This or another Collect is said

Almighty God,
in our baptism you have consecrated us
to be temples of your Holy Spirit.
May we, whom you have counted worthy,
nurture this gift of your indwelling Spirit with a lively faith
and worship you with upright lives;
through Jesus Christ our Lord.

All   **Amen.**

The water may be sprinkled over the people or they may be invited to use it to sign themselves with the cross.

The service ends either with the Peace or with the following blessing

May God, who in Christ gives us a spring of water
    welling up to eternal life,
perfect in you the image of his glory;
and may the blessing of God almighty,
the Father, the Son, and the Holy Spirit,
be among *you* and remain with *you* always.

All   **Amen.**

¶ *Thanksgiving*
for the Healing Ministry of the Church

See Note 8 on page 30.

Bless the Lord, O my soul;
All   **and forget not all his benefits.**

God forgives all our iniquities;
All   **and heals all our diseases.**

God redeems our life from the pit;
All   **and crowns us with love and mercy.**

James 5.13-16a or another suitable reading such as Mark 1.29-34 or Acts 3.1-10 follows.

This prayer of thanksgiving may be said

Blessed are you, sovereign God, gentle and merciful,
creator of heaven and earth.
Your word brought light out of darkness.
In Jesus Christ you proclaim good news to the poor,
liberty to captives, sight to the blind
and freedom for the oppressed.
Daily your Spirit renews the face of the earth,
bringing life and health, wholeness and peace.
In the renewal of our lives
you make known your heavenly glory.
Blessed be God, Father, Son and Holy Spirit:
All   **Blessed be God for ever.**

*The Apostles' Creed or an authorized Affirmation of Faith is said
at a principal service and may be said on other occasions (see Note 3).*

Intercessions for those in need and those who care for them may be offered in this or another form

Holy God, in whom we live and move and have our being,
we make our prayer to you, saying,
Lord, hear us.

All **Lord, graciously hear us.**

Grant to [*N and*] all who seek you
the assurance of your presence, your power and your peace.
Lord, hear us.

All **Lord, graciously hear us.**

Grant your healing grace to [*N and*] all who are sick
that they may be made whole in body, mind and spirit.
Lord, hear us.

All **Lord, graciously hear us.**

Grant to all who minister to the suffering
wisdom and skill, sympathy and patience.
Lord, hear us.

All **Lord, graciously hear us.**

Sustain and support the anxious and fearful
and lift up all who are brought low.
Lord, hear us.

All **Lord, graciously hear us.**

Hear us, Lord of life.

All **Heal us, and make us whole.**

This or another Collect is said

Almighty God,
whose Son revealed in signs and miracles
the wonder of your saving presence:
renew [*N, N, … and*] all your people
with your heavenly grace,
and in all our weakness
sustain us by your mighty power,
through Jesus Christ our Lord.

All **Amen.**

The Lord's Prayer is said.

The Ministry of Healing may take place here using these or other suitable prayers

Be with us, Spirit of God;

All **nothing can separate us from your love.**

Breathe on us, breath of God;

All **fill us with your saving power.**

Speak in us, wisdom of God;

All **bring strength, healing and peace.**

The Lord is here.

All **His Spirit is with us.**

Silence is kept.

If anointing is to be administered, a priest may use this prayer over the oil, if it has not previously been blessed

Lord, holy Father, giver of health and salvation,
as your apostles anointed those who were sick and healed them,
so continue the ministry of healing in your Church.
Sanctify this oil, that those who are anointed with it
may be freed from suffering and distress,
find inward peace, and know the joy of your salvation,
through your Son, our Saviour Jesus Christ.

All **Amen.**

The laying on of hands may be administered using these or other suitable words

In the name of God and trusting in his might alone,
receive Christ's healing touch to make you whole.

May Christ bring you wholeness of body, mind and spirit,
deliver you from every evil,
and give you his peace.

All **Amen.**

If anointing is administered by an authorized minister, these or other suitable words may be used

N, I anoint you in the name of God who gives you life.
Receive Christ's forgiveness, his healing and his love.

May the Father of our Lord Jesus Christ
grant you the riches of his grace,
his wholeness and his peace.

All **Amen.**

This prayer concludes the Ministry of Healing

The almighty Lord,
who is a strong tower for all who put their trust in him,
whom all things in heaven, on earth, and under the earth obey,
be now and evermore your defence.
May you believe and trust that the only name under heaven
given for health and salvation
is the name of our Lord Jesus Christ.

All **Amen.**

This responsory may be used

O magnify the Lord with me;
let us exalt his name together.

All **O magnify the Lord with me;
let us exalt his name together.**
I sought the Lord and he answered me;
he delivered me from all my fears.

All **O magnify the Lord with me.**
In my weakness I cried to the Lord;
he heard me and saved me from my troubles.

All **Let us exalt his name together.**
Glory to the Father, and to the Son
and to the Holy Spirit.

All **O magnify the Lord with me;
let us exalt his name together.** *cf Psalm 34*

The service ends with the Grace or a blessing or the Peace

Peace to you from God our Father who hears our cry.
Peace from his Son Jesus Christ whose death brings healing.
Peace from the Holy Spirit who gives us life and strength.
The peace of the Lord be always with you

All **and also with you.**

¶ *Thanksgiving for the Mission of the Church*

A suitable Gospel reading may be introduced by this acclamation

We proclaim not ourselves, but Christ Jesus as Lord

All **and ourselves as your servants for Jesus' sake.**

For the God who said, Let light shine out of darkness,

All **has caused the light to shine within us:**

to give the light of the knowledge of the glory of God

All **in the face of Jesus Christ.**

Hear the Gospel of our Lord Jesus Christ according to *N.*

All **Glory to you, O Lord.**

After the Gospel reading

This is the Gospel of the Lord.

All **Praise to you, O Christ.**

This prayer of thanksgiving may be said

Blessed are you,
the God and Father of our Lord Jesus Christ,
for you have blessed us in Christ with every spiritual blessing.
You chose us in Christ before the foundation of the world
and destined us for adoption as your children.
In Christ we have the forgiveness of sins,
an inheritance in your kingdom, the seal of your Spirit,
and in him we live for the praise of your glory
for ever and ever.

All **Amen.**

The commissioning of those called and prepared to exercise particular ministries may take place here.

The Apostles' Creed or an authorized Affirmation of Faith and this
affirmation of commitment are said at a principal service and may
be said on other occasions (see Note 3).

Will you continue in the apostles' teaching and fellowship,
in the breaking of bread, and in the prayers?

All **With the help of God, I will.**

Will you persevere in resisting evil,
and, whenever you fall into sin, repent and return to the Lord?

All **With the help of God, I will.**

Will you proclaim by word and example
the good news of God in Christ?

All **With the help of God, I will.**

Will you seek and serve Christ in all people,
loving your neighbour as yourself?

All **With the help of God, I will.**

Will you acknowledge Christ's authority over human society,
by prayer for the world and its leaders,
by defending the weak, and by seeking peace and justice?

All **With the help of God, I will.**

May Christ dwell in your hearts through faith,
that you may be rooted and grounded in love
and bring forth the fruit of the Spirit.

All **Amen.**

Intercessions for those engaged in ministry and other prayers
for the mission of the Church may be offered.

This Collect is said

Almighty God,
who called your Church to witness
that in Christ you were reconciling the world to yourself:
help us so to proclaim the good news of your love,
that all who hear it may be reconciled to you
through him who died for us and rose again
and reigns with you in the unity of the Holy Spirit,
one God, now and for ever.

All **Amen.**

The Lord's Prayer is said.

The service ends either with the Peace or with the following blessing

Let us bless the living God:
he was born of the Virgin Mary,

All **revealed in his glory,**
worshipped by angels,

All **proclaimed among the nations,**
believed in throughout the world,

All **exalted to the highest heavens.**

Blessed be God, our strength and our salvation,

All **now and for ever. Amen.**

Let us bless the Lord.

All **Thanks be to God.**

Notes to Orders for Morning and Evening Prayer on Sunday

In the services and the Notes square brackets indicate parts of the service which may be omitted.

1 **Hymns and Songs**
Hymns and songs may be sung at appropriate points in the service and metrical paraphrases may be used in place of the biblical canticles.

2 **Sentences of Scripture**
Alternative sentences of Scripture appropriate to the day or the season may be substituted for those in these orders.

3 Principal Services and Principal Holy Days

An authorized confession and absolution, and the Apostles' Creed or another Creed or authorized Affirmation of Faith, and a sermon, must be included in Morning or Evening Prayer when it is the principal service on a Sunday or Principal Holy Day, but may be omitted at other times. A Creed or authorized Affirmation of Faith is always used in the Thanksgiving for Holy Baptism. For further authorized forms of Confession and Absolution, and Creeds and authorized Affirmations of Faith, see *Common Worship: Services and Prayers for the Church of England* pages 122–152, 169–170 and 276–279.

4 Opening Canticle at Morning Prayer

The following are suitable for use as the opening canticle at Morning Prayer:

Benedicite – a Song of Creation (pages 38–39), especially in
    Ordinary Time;
Jubilate – a Song of Joy (page 41), especially in festal seasons;
The Easter Anthems (page 42), especially during the Easter season;
Venite – a Song of Triumph (page 40), especially during Advent
    and Lent.

5 Old and New Testament Canticles

The following are suitable as Old Testament canticles at Morning Prayer and New Testament canticles at Evening Prayer, especially in the seasons indicated:

	Morning	Evening
ent	A Song of the Wilderness (page 46)	A Song of the Spirit (page 52)
istmas	A Song of the Messiah (page 47)	A Song of Redemption (page 53)
phany	A Song of the New Jerusalem (page 48)	A Song of Praise (page 54)
t	A Song of Humility (page 49)	A Song of Christ the Servant (page 54)
ter	The Song of Moses and Miriam (page 50)	A Song of Faith (page 55)
tecost	A Song of Ezekiel (page 51)	A Song of God's Children (page 56)
inary Time	A Song of David (page 51)	A Song of the Lamb (page 56)

6 Opening Hymn and Canticle at Evening Prayer

Phos hilaron (A Song of the Light) is a suitable opening hymn (see page 43). Verses from either Psalm 104 or Psalm 141 are suitable opening canticles (see pages 44–45).

7   **Te Deum**
     The canticle Te Deum Laudamus – a Song of the Church (pages
     59–60), may be used at Morning or Evening Prayer immediately
     before the Conclusion.

8   **Thanksgivings**
     In Morning or Evening Prayer, one of the Thanksgivings may follow
     the sermon or, where a sermon is included in the Thanksgiving,
     the Gospel canticle. The confession and absolution at the beginning
     of Morning and Evening Prayer should be omitted where penitence
     is included in the Thanksgiving for the Word. If the Thanksgiving
     for the Healing Ministry of the Church is to include anointing,
     the minister must be authorized for this ministry as required by
     Canon B 37.

9   **Intercessions**
     These should normally be broadly based, expressing a concern for
     the whole of God's world and the ministry of the whole Church.
     Nevertheless, where occasion demands, they may be focused on
     more particular and local needs. Where another service follows
     immediately, they may be brief.

10   **Morning and Evening Collects**
     If it is desired to use the Morning and Evening Collects (page 31),
     they should not be added after the Collect of the Day, but should
     be used before the Blessing or other Ending.

11   **Commemoration of the Resurrection**
     The Order for Morning Prayer may be arranged as a
     commemoration of the resurrection (which is especially
     appropriate during the Easter season) by the use of the following:

     [*Opening Canticle*: Benedicite – a Song of Creation]
     Psalmody: Psalm 118.14-29
     [*First Reading*: Genesis 1.1-5; Exodus 14.21-31; 1 Corinthians 15.1-8
          or Colossians 3.1-4]
     Old Testament Canticle: The Song of Moses and Miriam
     Gospel Reading: Matthew 28.1-10; Mark 16.1-8; Mark 16.9-20;
          Luke 24.1-9; John 20.1-10; John 20.11-18; *or* John 21.1-14
     New Testament Canticle: The Easter Anthems

     For General Rules, see page 67.

Prayers for Various Occasions

A Morning Collect

Almighty and everlasting God,
we thank you that you have brought us safely
to the beginning of this day.
Keep us from falling into sin
or running into danger,
order us in all our doings
and guide us to do always
what is righteous in your sight;
through Jesus Christ our Lord.

All **Amen.**

An Evening Collect

Lighten our darkness,
Lord, we pray,
and in your great mercy
defend us from all perils and dangers of this night,
for the love of your only Son,
our Saviour Jesus Christ.

All **Amen.**

A Prayer for the Sovereign

Almighty God, the fountain of all goodness,
bless our Sovereign Lady, *Queen Elizabeth,*
and all who are in authority under her;
that they may order all things
in wisdom and equity, righteousness and peace,
to the honour of your name,
and the good of your Church and people;
through Jesus Christ our Lord.

All **Amen.**

A Prayer for the Royal Family

Almighty God, the fountain of all goodness,
bless, we pray, *Elizabeth the Queen Mother,*
Philip Duke of Edinburgh, Charles Prince of Wales,
and all the Royal Family.
Endue them with your Holy Spirit;
enrich them with your heavenly grace;
prosper them with all happiness;
and bring them to your everlasting kingdom;
through Jesus Christ our Lord.

All **Amen.**

A Prayer for Those who Govern

Eternal God,
fount and source of all authority and wisdom,
hear our prayer for those who govern.
Give to *Elizabeth our Queen* grace
as the symbol of loyalty and unity
for all our different peoples;
give to the parliaments in these islands,
and especially to our own Government,
wisdom and skill, imagination and energy;
give to the members of the European institutions
vision, understanding and integrity,
that all may live in peace and happiness, truth and prosperity;
through Jesus Christ our Lord.

All **Amen.**

A Prayer for Bishops and other Pastors

Almighty and everlasting God,
the only worker of great marvels,
send down upon our bishops and other pastors
and all congregations committed to their care
the spirit of your saving grace;
and that they may truly please you,
pour upon them the continual dew of your blessing.
Grant this, O Lord,
for the honour of our advocate and mediator, Jesus Christ.

All **Amen.**

All **Almighty God,**
     we thank you for the gift of your holy word.
     May it be a lantern to our feet,
     a light to our paths,
     and a strength to our lives.
     Take us and use us
     to love and serve
     in the power of the Holy Spirit
     and in the name of your Son,
     Jesus Christ our Lord.
     Amen.

A General Thanksgiving

     Almighty God, Father of all mercies,
     we thine unworthy servants
          do give thee most humble and hearty thanks
     for all thy goodness and loving-kindness to us and to all men;
 *   [*particularly to those who desire now to offer up their praises*
     and thanksgivings for thy late mercies vouchsafed unto them.]
     We bless thee for our creation, preservation,
          and all the blessings of this life;
     but above all for thine inestimable love
     in the redemption of the world by our Lord Jesus Christ,
     for the means of grace, and for the hope of glory.
     And we beseech thee, give us that due sense of all thy mercies,
     that our hearts may be unfeignedly thankful,
     and that we shew forth thy praise, not only with our lips,
          but in our lives;
     by giving up ourselves to thy service,
     and by walking before thee in holiness and righteousness
          all our days;
     through Jesus Christ our Lord,
     to whom with thee and the Holy Ghost
     be all honour and glory, world without end.
All **Amen.**

 *   *This to be said when any that have been prayed for*
     desire to return praise.

The Litany

Sections I and VII must always be used, but a selection of appropriate suffrages may be made from Sections II, III, IV, V and VI.

I

Let us pray.

God the Father,
All **have mercy upon us.**

God the Son,
All **have mercy upon us.**

God the Holy Spirit,
All **have mercy upon us.**

Holy, blessed and glorious Trinity,
All **have mercy upon us.**

II

From all evil and mischief;
from pride, vanity and hypocrisy;
from envy, hatred and malice;
and from all evil intent,
All **good Lord, deliver us.**

From sloth, worldliness and love of money;
from hardness of heart
and contempt for your word and your laws,
All **good Lord, deliver us.**

From sins of body and mind;
from the deceits of the world, the flesh and the devil,
All **good Lord, deliver us.**

From famine and disaster;
from violence, murder and dying unprepared,
All **good Lord, deliver us.**

In all times of sorrow;
in all times of joy;
in the hour of death,
and at the day of judgement,
All **good Lord, deliver us.**

III

By the mystery of your holy incarnation;
by your birth, childhood and obedience;
by your baptism, fasting and temptation,

All **good Lord, deliver us.**

By your ministry in word and work;
by your mighty acts of power;
and by your preaching of the kingdom,

All **good Lord, deliver us.**

By your agony and trial;
by your cross and passion;
and by your precious death and burial,

All **good Lord, deliver us.**

By your mighty resurrection;
by your glorious ascension;
and by your sending of the Holy Spirit,

All **good Lord, deliver us.**

IV

Hear our prayers, O Lord our God.

All **Hear us, good Lord.**

Govern and direct your holy Church;
fill it with love and truth;
and grant it that unity which is your will.

All **Hear us, good Lord.**

Give us boldness to preach the gospel in all the world,
and to make disciples of all the nations.

All **Hear us, good Lord.**

Enlighten *N* our Bishop and all who minister
with knowledge and understanding,
that by their teaching and their lives they may proclaim your word.

All **Hear us, good Lord.**

Give your people grace to hear and receive your word,
and to bring forth the fruit of the Spirit.

All **Hear us, good Lord.**

Bring into the way of truth all who have erred
and are deceived.

All **Hear us, good Lord.**

Strengthen those who stand;
comfort and help the faint-hearted;
raise up the fallen;
and finally beat down Satan under our feet.

All **Hear us, good Lord.**

V

Guide the leaders of the nations
into the ways of peace and justice.

All **Hear us, good Lord.**

Guard and strengthen your servant *Elizabeth our Queen*,
that she may put her trust in you,
and seek your honour and glory.

All **Hear us, good Lord.**

Endue the High Court of Parliament
and all the Ministers of the Crown
with wisdom and understanding.

All **Hear us, good Lord.**

Bless those who administer the law,
that they may uphold justice, honesty and truth.

All **Hear us, good Lord.**

Give us the will to use the resources of the earth to your glory,
and for the good of all creation.

All **Hear us, good Lord.**

Bless and keep all your people.

All **Hear us, good Lord.**

Bring your joy into all families;
strengthen and deliver those in childbirth,
watch over children and guide the young,
bring reconciliation to those in discord
and peace to those in stress.

All **Hear us, good Lord.**

VI

Help and comfort the lonely, the bereaved and the oppressed.

All **Lord, have mercy.**

Keep in safety those who travel, and all who are in danger.

All **Lord, have mercy.**

Heal the sick in body and mind,
and provide for the homeless, the hungry and the destitute.

All **Lord, have mercy.**

Show your pity on prisoners and refugees,
and all who are in trouble.

All **Lord, have mercy.**

Forgive our enemies, persecutors and slanderers,
and turn their hearts.

All **Lord, have mercy.**

Hear us as we remember
　　those who have died in the peace of Christ,
both those who have confessed the faith
and those whose faith is known to you alone,
and grant us with them a share in your eternal kingdom.

All **Lord, have mercy.**

VII

Give us true repentance;
forgive us our sins of negligence and ignorance
and our deliberate sins;
and grant us the grace of your Holy Spirit
to amend our lives according to your holy word.

All **Holy God,
holy and strong,
holy and immortal,
have mercy upon us.**

*When the Litany is said instead of the Prayers at Morning or
Evening Prayer, the Collect of the Day, the Lord's Prayer and the
Grace are added here.*

¶ *Opening Hymn and Canticles at Morning and Evening Prayer*

Benedicite – a Song of Creation

1   Bless the Lord all you works of the Lord: ◆
    sing his praise and exalt him for ever.

2   Bless the Lord you heavens: ◆
    sing his praise and exalt him for ever.

3   Bless the Lord you angels of the Lord: ◆
    bless the Lord all you his hosts;

    bless the Lord you waters above the heavens: ◆
    sing his praise and exalt him for ever.

4   Bless the Lord sun and moon: ◆
    bless the Lord you stars of heaven;

    bless the Lord all rain and dew: ◆
    sing his praise and exalt him for ever.

5   Bless the Lord all winds that blow: ◆
    bless the Lord you fire and heat;

    bless the Lord scorching wind and bitter cold: ◆
    sing his praise and exalt him for ever.

6   Bless the Lord dews and falling snows: ◆
    bless the Lord you nights and days;

    bless the Lord light and darkness: ◆
    sing his praise and exalt him for ever.

7   Bless the Lord frost and cold: ◆
    bless the Lord you ice and snow;

    bless the Lord lightnings and clouds: ◆
    sing his praise and exalt him for ever.

8   O let the earth bless the Lord: ◆
    bless the Lord you mountains and hills;

    bless the Lord all that grows in the ground: ◆
    sing his praise and exalt him for ever.

9   Bless the Lord you springs: ◆
    bless the Lord you seas and rivers;

bless the Lord you whales and all that swim in the waters: ♦
sing his praise and exalt him for ever.

10   Bless the Lord all birds of the air: ♦
bless the Lord you beasts and cattle;

bless the Lord all people on earth: ♦
sing his praise and exalt him for ever.

11   O people of God bless the Lord: ♦
bless the Lord you priests of the Lord;

bless the Lord you servants of the Lord: ♦
sing his praise and exalt him for ever.

12   Bless the Lord all you of upright spirit: ♦
bless the Lord you that are holy and humble in heart;

bless the Father, the Son and the Holy Spirit: ♦
sing his praise and exalt him for ever.

The Song of the Three 35-65

Benedicite – a Song of Creation
(shorter version)

1   Bless the Lord all you works of the Lord: ♦
sing his praise and exalt him for ever.

2   Bless the Lord you heavens: ♦
sing his praise and exalt him for ever.

3   Bless the Lord you angels of the Lord: ♦
sing his praise and exalt him for ever.

4   Bless the Lord all people on earth: ♦
sing his praise and exalt him for ever.

5   O people of God bless the Lord: ♦
sing his praise and exalt him for ever.

6   Bless the Lord you priests of the Lord: ♦
sing his praise and exalt him for ever.

7   Bless the Lord you servants of the Lord: ♦
sing his praise and exalt him for ever.

8   Bless the Lord all you of upright spirit: ♦
bless the Lord you that are holy and humble in heart;

bless the Father, the Son and the Holy Spirit: ♦
sing his praise and exalt him for ever.

1   O come, let us sing to the Lord; ♦
let us heartily rejoice in the rock of our salvation.

2   Let us come into his presence with thanksgiving ♦
and be glad in him with psalms.

3   For the Lord is a great God ♦
and a great king above all gods.

4   In his hand are the depths of the earth ♦
and the heights of the mountains are his also.

5   The sea is his, for he made it, ♦
and his hands have moulded the dry land.

6   Come, let us worship and bow down ♦
and kneel before the Lord our Maker.

7   For he is our God; ♦
we are the people of his pasture and the sheep of his hand.

The canticle may end here with 'Glory to the Father…'

8   O that today you would listen to his voice: ♦
'Harden not your hearts as at Meribah,
    on that day at Massah in the wilderness,

9   'When your forebears tested me, and put me to the proof, ♦
though they had seen my works.

10   'Forty years long I detested that generation and said, ♦
"This people are wayward in their hearts;
    they do not know my ways."

11   'So I swore in my wrath, ♦
"They shall not enter into my rest." '   *Psalm 95*

Glory to the Father and to the Son
and to the Holy Spirit;
as it was in the beginning is now
and shall be for ever. Amen.

Jubilate – a Song of Joy

1 O be joyful in the Lord, all the earth; ♦
   serve the Lord with gladness
        and come before his presence with a song.

2 Know that the Lord is God; ♦
   it is he that has made us and we are his;
        we are his people and the sheep of his pasture.

3 Enter his gates with thanksgiving
        and his courts with praise; ♦
   give thanks to him and bless his name.

4 For the Lord is gracious; his steadfast love is everlasting, ♦
   and his faithfulness endures from generation to generation.

Psalm 100

   Glory to the Father and to the Son
   and to the Holy Spirit;
   as it was in the beginning is now
   and shall be for ever. Amen.

1   Christ our passover has been sacrificed for us: ◆
    so let us celebrate the feast,

2   not with the old leaven of corruption and wickedness: ◆
    but with the unleavened bread of sincerity and truth.

1 Corinthians 5.7

3   Christ once raised from the dead dies no more: ◆
    death has no more dominion over him.

4   In dying he died to sin once for all: ◆
    in living he lives to God.

5   See yourselves therefore as dead to sin: ◆
    and alive to God in Jesus Christ our Lord.   *Romans 6.9*

6   Christ has been raised from the dead: ◆
    the first fruits of those who sleep.

7   For as by man came death: ◆
    by man has come also the resurrection of the dead;

8   for as in Adam all die: ◆
    even so in Christ shall all be made alive.   *1 Corinthians 15.20*

    Glory to the Father and to the Son
    and to the Holy Spirit;
    as it was in the beginning is now
    and shall be for ever. Amen.

Evening Prayer

Phos hilaron – a Song of the Light

O joyful light,
from the pure glory of the eternal heavenly Father,
O holy, blessed Jesus Christ.

As we come to the setting of the sun
and see the evening light,
we give thanks and praise to the Father and to the Son
and to the Holy Spirit of God.

Worthy are you at all times
to be sung with holy voices,
O Son of God, O giver of life,
and to be glorified through all creation.

(or)

Hail, gladdening Light, of his pure glory poured,
Who is the immortal Father, heavenly, blest,
Holiest of holies, Jesus Christ our Lord.

Now we are come to the sun's hour of rest,
The lights of evening round us shine,
We hymn the Father, Son and Holy Spirit divine.

Worthy are you at all times to be sung
With undefiled tongue,
Son of our God, giver of life, alone:
Therefore in all the world your glories, Lord, they own.

All **Let my prayer rise before you as incense, ♦
the lifting up of my hands as the evening sacrifice.**

O Lord, I call to you; come to me quickly; ♦
hear my voice when I cry to you.

Set a watch before my mouth, O Lord, ♦
and guard the door of my lips;

All **Let my prayer rise before you as incense, ♦
the lifting up of my hands as the evening sacrifice.**

Let not my heart incline to any evil thing; ♦
let me not be occupied in wickedness with evildoers.

But my eyes are turned to you, Lord God; ♦
in you I take refuge; do not leave me defenceless.

All **Let my prayer rise before you as incense, ♦
the lifting up of my hands as the evening sacrifice.**

Verses from Psalm 104

All **Bless the Lord, O my soul. ♦**
O Lord my God, how excellent is your greatness!

You are clothed with majesty and honour, ♦
wrapped in light as in a garment.

The sun knows the time for its setting. ♦
You make darkness that it may be night.

All **Bless the Lord, O my soul. ♦**
O Lord my God, how excellent is your greatness!

O Lord, how manifold are your works! ♦
In wisdom you have made them all;
    the earth is full of your creatures.

When you send forth your spirit, they are created, ♦
and you renew the face of the earth.

All **Bless the Lord, O my soul. ♦**
O Lord my God, how excellent is your greatness!

May the glory of the Lord endure for ever; ♦
may the Lord rejoice in his works;

I will sing to the Lord as long as I live; ♦
I will make music to my God while I have my being.

All **Bless the Lord, O my soul. ♦**
O Lord my God, how excellent is your greatness!

¶ *Old and New Testament Canticles at Morning and Evening Prayer*

Morning Prayer

A Song of the Wilderness (Advent)

1   The wilderness and the dry land shall rejoice, ♦
    the desert shall blossom and burst into song.

2   They shall see the glory of the Lord, ♦
    the majesty of our God.

3   Strengthen the weary hands, ♦
    and make firm the feeble knees.

4   Say to the anxious, 'Be strong, fear not,
        your God is coming with judgement, ♦
    coming with judgement to save you.'

5   Then shall the eyes of the blind be opened, ♦
    and the ears of the deaf unstopped;

6   Then shall the lame leap like a hart, ♦
    and the tongue of the dumb sing for joy.

7   For waters shall break forth in the wilderness, ♦
    and streams in the desert;

8   The ransomed of the Lord shall return with singing, ♦
    with everlasting joy upon their heads.

9   Joy and gladness shall be theirs, ♦
    and sorrow and sighing shall flee away.   *Isaiah 35.1,2b-4a,4c-6*

    Glory to the Father and to the Son
    and to the Holy Spirit;
    as it was in the beginning is now
    and shall be for ever. Amen.

A Song of the Messiah (Christmas)

1   The people who walked in darkness have seen a great light; ♦
     those who dwelt in a land of deep darkness,
       upon them the light has dawned.

2   You have increased their joy and given them great gladness; ♦
     they rejoiced before you as with joy at the harvest.

3   For you have shattered the yoke that burdened them; ♦
     the collar that lay heavy on their shoulders.

4   For to us a child is born and to us a son is given, ♦
     and the government will be upon his shoulder.

5   And his name will be called: Wonderful Counsellor;
       the Mighty God; ♦
     the Everlasting Father; the Prince of Peace.

6   Of the increase of his government and of peace ♦
     there will be no end,

7   Upon the throne of David and over his kingdom, ♦
     to establish and uphold it with justice and righteousness.

8   From this time forth and for evermore; ♦
     the zeal of the Lord of hosts will do this.   *Isaiah 9.2,3b,4a,6,7*

Glory to the Father and to the Son
and to the Holy Spirit;
as it was in the beginning is now
and shall be for ever. Amen.

A Song of the New Jerusalem (Epiphany)

1   Arise, shine out, for your light has come, ♦
       the glory of the Lord is rising upon you.

2   Though night still covers the earth, ♦
       and darkness the peoples;

3   Above you the Holy One arises, ♦
       and above you God's glory appears.

4   The nations will come to your light, ♦
       and kings to your dawning brightness.

5   Your gates will lie open continually, ♦
       shut neither by day nor by night.

6   The sound of violence shall be heard no longer in your land, ♦
       or ruin and devastation within your borders.

7   You will call your walls, Salvation, ♦
       and your gates, Praise.

8   No more will the sun give you daylight, ♦
       nor moonlight shine upon you;

9   But the Lord will be your everlasting light, ♦
       your God will be your splendour,

10   For you shall be called the city of God, ♦
       the dwelling of the Holy One of Israel.   *Isaiah 60.1-3,11a,18,19,*

       Glory to the Father and to the Son
       and to the Holy Spirit;
       as it was in the beginning is now
       and shall be for ever. Amen.

A Song of Humility (Lent)

1   Come, let us return to the Lord ♦
    who has torn us and will heal us.

2   God has stricken us ♦
    and will bind up our wounds.

3   After two days, he will revive us, ♦
    and on the third day will raise us up,
        that we may live in his presence.

4   Let us strive to know the Lord; ♦
    his appearing is as sure as the sunrise.

5   He will come to us like the showers, ♦
    like the spring rains that water the earth.

6   'O Ephraim, how shall I deal with you? ♦
    How shall I deal with you, O Judah?

7   'Your love for me is like the morning mist, ♦
    like the dew that goes early away.

8   'Therefore, I have hewn them by the prophets, ♦
    and my judgement goes forth as the light.

9   'For loyalty is my desire and not sacrifice, ♦
    and the knowledge of God rather than burnt offerings.'   *Hosea 6.1-6*

    Glory to the Father and to the Son
    and to the Holy Spirit;
    as it was in the beginning is now
    and shall be for ever. Amen.

The Song of Moses and Miriam (Easter)

1   I will sing to the Lord, who has triumphed gloriously, ♦
    the horse and his rider he has thrown into the sea.

2   The Lord is my strength and my song ♦
    and has become my salvation.

3   This is my God whom I will praise, ♦
    the God of my forebears whom I will exalt.

4   The Lord is a warrior, ♦
    the Lord is his name.

5   Your right hand, O Lord, is glorious in power: ♦
    your right hand, O Lord, shatters the enemy.

6   At the blast of your nostrils, the sea covered them; ♦
    they sank as lead in the mighty waters.

7   In your unfailing love, O Lord, ♦
    you lead the people whom you have redeemed.

8   And by your invincible strength ♦
    you will guide them to your holy dwelling.

9   You will bring them in and plant them, O Lord, ♦
    in the sanctuary which your hands have established.

Exodus 15.1b-3,6,10,13,

Glory to the Father and to the Son
and to the Holy Spirit;
as it was in the beginning is now
and shall be for ever. Amen.

A Song of Ezekiel (Pentecost)

1 I will take you from the nations, ♦
  and gather you from all the countries.

2 I will sprinkle clean water upon you, ♦
  and you shall be clean from all your uncleannesses.

3 A new heart I will give you, ♦
  and put a new spirit within you,

4 And I will remove from your body the heart of stone ♦
  and give you a heart of flesh.

5 You shall be my people, ♦
  and I will be your God.   *Ezekiel 36.24-26,28b*

  Glory to the Father and to the Son
  and to the Holy Spirit;
  as it was in the beginning is now
  and shall be for ever. Amen.

A Song of David (Ordinary Time)

1 Blessed are you, God of Israel, for ever and ever, ♦
  for yours is the greatness, the power,
     the glory, the splendour and the majesty.

2 Everything in heaven and on earth is yours; ♦
  yours is the kingdom, O Lord,
     and you are exalted as head over all.

3 Riches and honour come from you ♦
  and you rule over all.

4 In your hand are power and might; ♦
  yours it is to give power and strength to all.

5 And now we give you thanks, our God, ♦
  and praise your glorious name.

6 For all things come from you, ♦
  and of your own have we given you.   *I Chronicles 29.10b-13,14b*

  Glory to the Father and to the Son
  and to the Holy Spirit;
  as it was in the beginning is now
  and shall be for ever. Amen.

Evening Prayer

A Song of the Spirit (Advent)

1   'Behold, I am coming soon', says the Lord,
        'and bringing my reward with me, ✦
    to give to everyone according to their deeds.

2   'I am the Alpha and the Omega, the first and the last, ✦
    the beginning and the end.'

3   Blessed are those who do God's commandments,
        that they may have the right to the tree of life, ✦
    and may enter into the city through the gates.

4   'I, Jesus, have sent my angel to you, ✦
    with this testimony for all the churches.

5   'I am the root and the offspring of David, ✦
    I am the bright morning star.'

6   'Come!' say the Spirit and the Bride; ✦
    'Come!' let each hearer reply!

7   Come forward, you who are thirsty, ✦
    let those who desire take the water of life as a gift.

Revelation 22.12-14, 16, ✦

Surely I am coming soon! ✦
Amen! Come, Lord Jesus!

A Song of Redemption (Christmas)

1   The Father has delivered us from the dominion of darkness, ♦
    and transferred us to the kingdom of his beloved Son;

2   In whom we have redemption, ♦
    the forgiveness of our sins.

3   He is the image of the invisible God, ♦
    the firstborn of all creation.

4   For in him all things were created, ♦
    in heaven and on earth, visible and invisible.

5   All things were created through him and for him, ♦
    he is before all things and in him all things hold together.

6   He is the head of the body, the Church, ♦
    he is the beginning, the firstborn from the dead.

7   In him all the fullness of God was pleased to dwell; ♦
    and through him God was pleased to reconcile all things.

Colossians 1.13-18a, 19, 20a

Glory to the Father and to the Son
and to the Holy Spirit;
as it was in the beginning is now
and shall be for ever. Amen.

A Song of Praise (Epiphany)

This Canticle is also known as Glory and Honour.

1   You are worthy, our Lord and God, ♦
    to receive glory and honour and power.

2   For you have created all things, ♦
    and by your will they have their being.

3   You are worthy, O Lamb, for you were slain, ♦
    and by your blood you ransomed for God
        saints from every tribe and language and nation.

4   You have made them to be a kingdom and priests
        serving our God, ♦
    and they will reign with you on earth.   *Revelation 4.11; 5.9b,*

    To the One who sits on the throne and to the Lamb ♦
    be blessing and honour, glory and might,
        for ever and ever. Amen.

A Song of Christ the Servant (Lent)

1   Christ suffered for you, leaving you an example, ♦
    that you should follow in his steps.

2   He committed no sin, no guile was found on his lips, ♦
    when he was reviled, he did not revile in turn.

3   When he suffered, he did not threaten, ♦
    but he trusted himself to God who judges justly.

4   Christ himself bore our sins in his body on the tree, ♦
    that we might die to sin and live to righteousness.

5   By his wounds, you have been healed,
        for you were straying like sheep, ♦
    but have now returned
        to the shepherd and guardian of your souls.   *1 Peter 2.21b-2*

    Glory to the Father and to the Son
    and to the Holy Spirit;
    as it was in the beginning is now
    and shall be for ever. Amen.

A Song of Faith (Easter)

1   Blessed be the God and Father ♦
     of our Lord Jesus Christ!

2   By his great mercy we have been born anew to a living hope ♦
     through the resurrection of Jesus Christ from the dead,

3   Into an inheritance that is imperishable, undefiled and unfading, ♦
     kept in heaven for you,

4   Who are being protected by the power of God
       through faith for a salvation, ♦
     ready to be revealed in the last time.

5   You were ransomed from the futile ways of your ancestors ♦
     not with perishable things like silver or gold

6   But with the precious blood of Christ ♦
     like that of a lamb without spot or stain.

7   Through him we have confidence in God,
       who raised him from the dead and gave him glory, ♦
     so that your faith and hope are set on God.   *1 Peter 1.3-5,18,19,21*

Glory to the Father and to the Son
and to the Holy Spirit;
as it was in the beginning is now
and shall be for ever.   Amen.

A Song of God's Children (Pentecost)

1   The law of the Spirit of life in Christ Jesus ♦
       has set us free from the law of sin and death.

2   All who are led by the Spirit of God are children of God; ♦
       for we have received the Spirit that enables us to cry, 'Abba, Father

3   The Spirit himself bears witness that we are children of God ♦
       and if God's children, then heirs of God;

4   If heirs of God, then fellow-heirs with Christ; ♦
       since we suffer with him now, that we may be glorified with him.

5   These sufferings that we now endure ♦
       are not worth comparing to the glory that shall be revealed.

6   For the creation waits with eager longing ♦
       for the revealing of the children of God.   *Romans 8.2,14,15b-*

       Glory to the Father and to the Son
       and to the Holy Spirit;
       as it was in the beginning is now
       and shall be for ever.   Amen.

A Song of the Lamb (Ordinary Time)

1   Salvation and glory and power belong to our God, ♦
       whose judgements are true and just.

2   Praise our God, all you his servants, ♦
       all who fear him, both small and great.

3   The Lord our God, the Almighty, reigns: ♦
       let us rejoice and exult and give him the glory.

4   For the marriage of the Lamb has come ♦
       and his bride has made herself ready.

5   Blessed are those who are invited ♦
       to the wedding banquet of the Lamb.   *Revelation 19.1b,5b,6b,7,*

       To the One who sits on the throne and to the Lamb ♦
       be blessing and honour and glory and might,
          for ever and ever.   Amen.

¶ *Other Canticles*

Nunc dimittis (The Song of Simeon)

1   Now, Lord, you let your servant go in peace: ♦
    your word has been fulfilled.

2   My own eyes have seen the salvation ♦
    which you have prepared in the sight of every people;

3   A light to reveal you to the nations ♦
    and the glory of your people Israel.   *Luke 2.29-32*

    Glory to the Father and to the Son
    and to the Holy Spirit;
    as it was in the beginning is now
    and shall be for ever. Amen.

The Song of Christ's Glory

1   Christ Jesus was in the form of God, ♦
    but he did not cling to equality with God.

2   He emptied himself, taking the form of a servant, ♦
    and was born in our human likeness.

3   Being found in human form he humbled himself, ♦
    and became obedient unto death, even death on a cross.

4   Therefore God has highly exalted him, ♦
    and bestowed on him the name above every name,

5   That at the name of Jesus, every knee should bow, ♦
    in heaven and on earth and under the earth;

6   And every tongue confess that Jesus Christ is Lord, ♦
    to the glory of God the Father.   *Philippians 2.5-11*

    Glory to the Father and to the Son
    and to the Holy Spirit;
    as it was in the beginning is now
    and shall be for ever. Amen.

Great and Wonderful

1   Great and wonderful are your deeds, ♦
    Lord God the Almighty.

2   Just and true are your ways, ♦
    O ruler of the nations.

3   Who shall not revere and praise your name, O Lord? ♦
    for you alone are holy.

4   All nations shall come and worship in your presence: ♦
    for your just dealings have been revealed.   *Revelation 15.3*

To the One who sits on the throne and to the Lamb ♦
be blessing and honour and glory and might,
    for ever and ever. Amen.

Bless the Lord

1   Blessed are you, the God of our ancestors, ♦
    worthy to be praised and exalted for ever.

2   Blessed is your holy and glorious name, ♦
    worthy to be praised and exalted for ever.

3   Blessed are you, in your holy and glorious temple, ♦
    worthy to be praised and exalted for ever.

4   Blessed are you who look into the depths, ♦
    worthy to be praised and exalted for ever.

5   Blessed are you, enthroned on the cherubim, ♦
    worthy to be praised and exalted for ever.

6   Blessed are you on the throne of your kingdom, ♦
    worthy to be praised and exalted for ever.

7   Blessed are you in the heights of heaven, ♦
    worthy to be praised and exalted for ever.

The Song of the Three 29-

Bless the Father, the Son and the Holy Spirit,
worthy to be praised and exalted for ever.

1   Jesus, Saviour of the world,
        come to us in your mercy: ♦
    we look to you to save and help us.

2   By your cross and your life laid down,
        you set your people free: ♦
    we look to you to save and help us.

3   When they were ready to perish, you saved your disciples: ♦
    we look to you to come to our help.

4   In the greatness of your mercy, loose us from our chains, ♦
    forgive the sins of all your people.

5   Make yourself known as our Saviour and mighty deliverer; ♦
    save and help us that we may praise you.

6   Come now and dwell with us, Lord Christ Jesus: ♦
    hear our prayer and be with us always.

7   And when you come in your glory: ♦
    make us to be one with you
        and to share the life of your kingdom.

¶ *Te Deum Laudamus*

See Note 7, page 30.

We praise you, O God,
we acclaim you as the Lord;
all creation worships you,
the Father everlasting.
To you all angels, all the powers of heaven,
the cherubim and seraphim, sing in endless praise:
Holy, holy, holy Lord, God of power and might,
heaven and earth are full of your glory.
The glorious company of apostles praise you.
The noble fellowship of prophets praise you.
The white-robed army of martyrs praise you.
Throughout the world the holy Church acclaims you:
Father, of majesty unbounded,
your true and only Son, worthy of all praise,
the Holy Spirit, advocate and guide.

You, Christ, are the King of glory,
the eternal Son of the Father.
When you took our flesh to set us free
you humbly chose the Virgin's womb.
You overcame the sting of death
and opened the kingdom of heaven to all believers.
You are seated at God's right hand in glory.
We believe that you will come and be our judge.
Come then, Lord, and help your people,
bought with the price of your own blood,
and bring us with your saints
to glory everlasting.

The canticle may end here.

Save your people, Lord, and bless your inheritance.
Govern and uphold them now and always.

Day by day we bless you.
We praise your name for ever.

Keep us today, Lord, from all sin.
Have mercy on us, Lord, have mercy.

Lord, show us your love and mercy,
for we have put our trust in you.

In you, Lord, is our hope:
let us never be put to shame.

A Service of the Word

¶ *Introduction*

A Service of the Word is unusual for an authorized Church of England service. It consists almost entirely of notes and directions and allows for considerable local variation and choice within a common structure. It is important that those who prepare for and take part in A Service of the Word should have a clear understanding of the nature of worship and of how the component parts of this service work together. Leading people in worship is leading people into mystery, into the unknown and yet the familiar. This spiritual activity is much more than getting the words or the sections in the right order. The primary object in the careful planning and leading of the service is the spiritual direction which enables the whole congregation to come into the presence of God to give him glory. Choices must be made responsibly by leaders of this service or by groups planning worship with them, whether the service is an occasional one, or a regular one which may use a service card. The notes and the text of A Service of the Word should be read together as they interpret one another.

The Liturgy of the Word

At the heart of the service is the Liturgy of the Word. This must not be so lightly treated as to appear insignificant compared with other parts of the service. The readings from Holy Scripture are central to this part and, together with the season, may determine the theme of the rest of the worship. At certain times of the year, as Note 5 says, the readings come from an authorized lectionary, so that the whole Church is together proclaiming the major events in the Christian story. Telling that story and expounding it in the 'sermon' can be done in many different and adventurous ways. Some are suggested in Notes 5 and 7, but there are many others. The word 'sermon' is used in the service, and explained in the note, precisely because it would be too limiting to use words like 'address', 'talk', 'instruction', or 'meditation'.

The items in the Liturgy of the Word may come in any order and more than once. So the sermon may be in parts and there may be more than one psalm or song, and of course hymns may be inserted as well. But on most occasions it will be appropriate for this part of the service to have a Creed or Affirmation of Faith as its climax. (See pages 138–152 of *Common Worship: Services and Prayers for the Church of England*.)

Preparation

With the Liturgy of the Word becoming clear it will be easier to see how the Preparation for it, and the response to it in the Prayers, fit in. People need to know when the service has started (Note 1). What happens at the beginning can create the atmosphere for worship and set the tone and mood for what follows. The gathering of the congregation and the call to worship are to be marked by a liturgical greeting between minister and people. Leaders should have worked out exactly where this comes among the singing, Scripture sentence, introduction (perhaps to the theme) and opening prayer. All these should draw the members of the congregation together and focus their attention on almighty God.

This part of the service will usually include the Prayers of Penitence though these may come later if, for instance, the theme of the Liturgy of the Word appropriately leads to penitence. Authorized Prayers of Penitence include all those confessions and absolutions in *The Book of Common Prayer* and in services in *Common Worship*, together with several other seasonal and thematic forms, mostly for occasional use, which are set out on pages 122–137 in *Common Worship: Services and Prayers for the Church of England*. The climax of this part of the service is either the Collect or, if that is included in the Prayers, one of the items of praise, a hymn or the Gloria. The Collect does not have to be that of the day; it may be a thematic one based on the readings (in which case it should come immediately before the readings), or be used to sum up the Prayer

Prayers

Part of the response to the Word is the Creed, but the response should be developed in the Prayers which follow. There are many different options for this part of the service. These range from a series of Collect-type prayers to congregational involvement in prayer groups, visual and processional prayers, with responsive forms and a number of people sharing the leading of intercessions in between. But, whatever the form, it is essential that the Prayers also include thanksgiving. A section of thanksgiving, which may include the spoken word, music and hymns, may be the proper climax to this part of the service.

Conclusion

Many different words have been used for the Conclusion, each of which has something to contribute to our understanding of how the service ends: dismissal, farewell, goodbye, departure, valediction, commission, blessing, ending, going out. What is essential, as with the way the service starts, is that it should have a clear liturgical ending: options are listed in Note 9.

Once the service is planned, leaders will want to check through to ensure that there is the right balance between the elements of word, prayer and praise, and between congregational activity and congregational passivity. Does the music come in the right places? Is there sufficient silence (Note 4)? This is something leaders can be afraid of, or fail to introduce properly. And is there a clear overall direction to the service: is it achieving the purpose of bringing the congregation together to give glory to God?

¶ A Service of the Word

The minister welcomes the people with the **Greeting**.

Authorized Prayers of Penitence may be used here or in the **Prayers**.

The Venite, Kyries, Gloria, a hymn, song, or a set of responses may be used.

The **Collect** is said either here or in the **Prayers**.

The Liturgy of the Word

This includes
- ¶ **readings (or a reading) from Holy Scripture**
- ¶ a **psalm**, or, if occasion demands, a scriptural song
- ¶ a **sermon**
- ¶ an **authorized Creed**, or, if occasion demands, an **authorized Affirmation of Faith.**

Prayers

These include
- ¶ **intercessions and thanksgivings**
- ¶ **the Lord's Prayer**

Conclusion

The service concludes with a **blessing, dismissal** or other **liturgical ending**.

For a Service of the Word with a Celebration of Holy Communion, see page 25 of Common Worship: Services and Prayers for the Church of England.

¶ Notes

In this form of service, the material is described as 'authorized' or 'suitable', which expressions shall have the following meanings:

¶ 'authorized' means approved by the General Synod in accordance with the provisions of Canon B 2.

¶ 'suitable' means a form used at the discretion of the minister conducting the form of service on any occasion, but such that the material so used shall be neither contrary to, nor indicative of any departure from, the doctrine of the Church of England in any essential matter.

This service is authorized as an alternative to Morning Prayer and Evening Prayer. It provides a structure for Sunday services, for daily prayer and for services of an occasional nature.

1   **Greeting**
The service should have a clear beginning. The liturgical greeting may follow some introductory singing, or a hymn or a sentence of Scripture, and may be followed by a brief introduction or an opening prayer.

2   **Prayers of Penitence**
Only authorized Prayers of Penitence should be used. They may be omitted except at the Principal Service on Sundays and Principal Holy Days. Authorized forms of Confession and Absolution may be found in *The Book of Common Prayer*, in the services in *Common Worship* and on pages 122–137 *of Common Worship: Services and Prayers for the Church of England*. The minister may introduce the Confession with suitable words.

3   **Hymns, Canticles, Acclamations and the Peace**
Points are indicated for some of these, but if occasion requires they may occur elsewhere.

4   **Silence**
Periods of silence may be kept at different points of the service. It may be particularly appropriate at the beginning of the service, after the readings and the sermon, and during the prayers.

5   **Readings**
There should preferably be at least two readings from the Bible, but it is recognized that if occasion demands there may be only

one reading. It may be dramatized, sung or read responsively. The readings are taken from an authorized lectionary during the period from the Third Sunday of Advent to the Baptism of Christ, and from Palm Sunday to Trinity Sunday. When A Service of the Word is combined with Holy Communion on Sundays and Princip Holy Days, the readings of the day are normally used.

6 **Psalms**

The service should normally include a psalm or psalms. These mig be said or sung in the traditional way, but it is also possible to use metrical version, a responsive form or a paraphrase such as can be found in many current hymn books. The psalm may occasionally b replaced by a song or canticle the words of which are taken direc from Scripture: a 'scriptural song'.

7 **Sermon**

The term 'sermon' includes less formal exposition, the use of dra interviews, discussion, audio-visuals and the insertion of hymns or other sections of the service between parts of the sermon. The sermon may come after one of the readings, or before or after the prayers, and may be omitted except on Sundays and Principal Holy Days.

8 **Sermon and Creed**

The sermon, and a Creed or authorized Affirmation of Faith may omitted except at the principal service on Sundays and Principal Holy Days.

9 **Ending**

The service should have a clear ending. This takes one or more of the following forms: the Peace, the Grace or a suitable ascription or blessing. If a responsive conclusion is used, it comes last.

10 **A Service of the Word with a Celebration of Holy Communi**

An order for this is provided (see page 25 of *Common Worship: Servi and Prayers for the Church of England*). The notes to the Order for th Celebration of Holy Communion (pages 158–159 and 330–335 of *Common Worship: Services and Prayers for the Church of England*) appl equally to this service. In particular the Note on Ministries specifies that the president must be an episcopally ordained priest, but indic that where necessary a deacon or lay person may preside over the Preparation and the Liturgy of the Word, including the Prayers. The order provided is not prescriptive.

General Rules for Regulating Authorized Forms of Service

1   Any reference in authorized provision to the use of hymns shall be construed as including the use of texts described as songs, chants, canticles.

2   If occasion requires, hymns may be sung at points other than those indicated in particular forms of service. Silence may be kept at points other than those indicated in particular forms of service.

3   Where rubrics indicate that a text is to be 'said' this must be understood to include 'or sung' and vice versa.

4   Where parts of a service make use of well-known and traditional texts, other translations or versions, particularly when used in musical compositions, may be used.

5   Local custom may be established and followed in respect of posture but regard should be had to indications in Notes attached to authorized forms of service that a particular posture is appropriate for some parts of that form of service.

6   On any occasion when the text of an alternative service authorized under the provisions of Canon B 2 provides for the Lord's Prayer to be said or sung, it may be used in the form included in *The Book of Common Prayer* or in either of the two other forms included in services in *Common Worship*. The further text included in Prayers for Various Occasions (page 106 in *Common Worship: Services and Prayers for the Church of England*) may be used on suitable occasions.

7   Normally on any occasion only one Collect is used.

8   At Baptisms, Confirmations, Ordinations and Marriages which take place on Principal Feasts, other Principal Holy Days and on Sundays of Advent, Lent and Easter, within the Celebration of the Holy Communion, the Readings of the day are used and the Collect of the Day is said, unless the bishop directs otherwise.

9   The Collects and Lectionary in *Common Worship* may, optionally, be used in conjunction with the days included in the Calendar of *The Book of Common Prayer*, notwithstanding any difference in the title or name of a Sunday, Holy Day or other observance included in both Calendars.

Acknowledgements

The publisher gratefully acknowledges permission to reproduce copyright material in this book. Every effort has been made to trace and contact copyright holders. If there are any inadvertent omissions we apologize to those concerned and undertake to include suitable acknowledgements in all future editions.

Published sources include the following:

Cambridge University Press: extracts (and adapted extracts) from *The Book of Common Prayer*, the rights in which are vested in the Crown, are reproduced by permission of the Crown's Patentee, Cambridge University Press.

The English Language Liturgical Consultation: English translation of the Lord's Prayer and the Apostles' Creed prepared by the English Language Liturgical Consultation, based on (or excerpted from) *Praying Together* © ELLC 1988.

The European Province of the Society of St Francis: adapted extracts from *Celebrating Common Prayer* © The Society of St Francis European Province 1992 and 1996.